SCIENTIST'S
TOOLS

ANDERS HANSON

Consulting Editor, Diane Craig, M.A./Reading Specialist

A Division of ABDO

ABDO
Publishing Company

visit us at www.abdopublishing.com

Published by ABDO Publishing Company, a division of ABDO,
P.O. Box 398166, Minneapolis, Minnesota 55439. Copyright © 2011
by Abdo Consulting Group, Inc. International copyrights reserved in
all countries. No part of this book may be reproduced in any form
without written permission from the publisher. Super SandCastle™
is a trademark and logo of ABDO Publishing Company.

Printed in the United States of America,
North Mankato, Minnesota
092010
012011

Editor: Liz Salzmann
Content Developer: Nancy Tuminelly
Photo Credits: Shutterstock

Library of Congress Cataloging-in-Publication Data

Hanson, Anders, 1980-
  Scientist's tools / Anders Hanson.
    p. cm. -- (Professional tools)
  ISBN 978-1-61613-581-2
  1. Scientific apparatus and instruments--Juvenile literature. 2.
Scientists--Juvenile literature. I. Title.
  Q185.3.H36 2011
  502.8--dc22
                        2010018610

Super SandCastle™ books are created by a team of professional
educators, reading specialists, and content developers around
five essential components—phonemic awareness, phonics,
vocabulary, text comprehension, and fluency—to assist young
readers as they develop reading skills and strategies and
increase their general knowledge. All books are written,
reviewed, and leveled for guided reading, early reading
intervention, and Accelerated Reader® programs for use in
shared, guided, and independent reading and writing activities to
support a balanced approach to literacy instruction.

CONTENTS

MEET A SCIENTIST

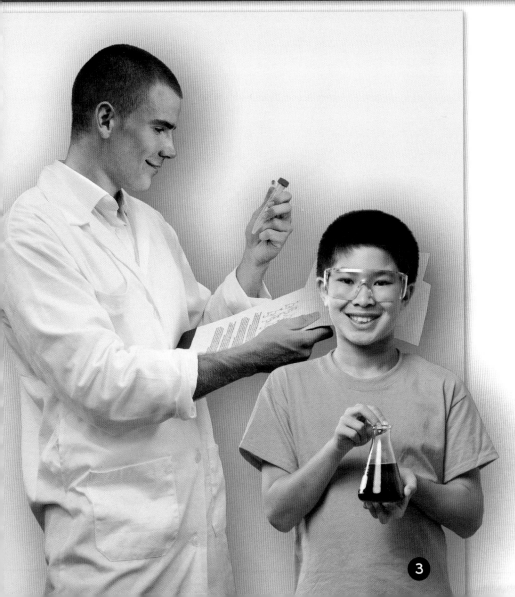

WHAT DOES A SCIENTIST DO?

Scientists do experiments to learn how things work. There are many kinds of scientists. Chemists and astronomers are scientists.

WHY DO SCIENTISTS NEED TOOLS?

Scientists use special tools to look at, listen to, and measure things. Some tools make things that are tiny look big. Other tools measure exactly how much of something there is.

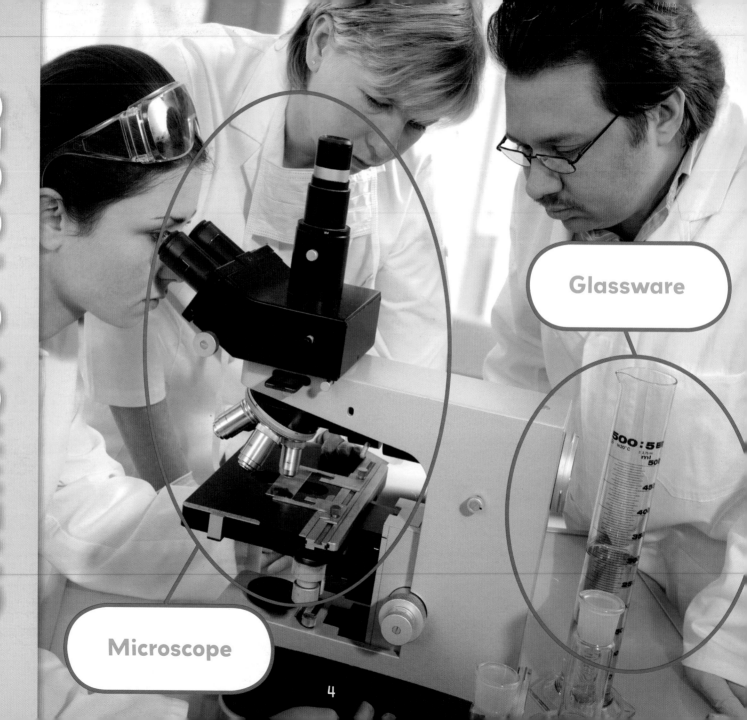

Glassware

Microscope

Radio Telescope

Optical Telescope

ASTRONOMER'S TOOLS

5

MICROSCOPE

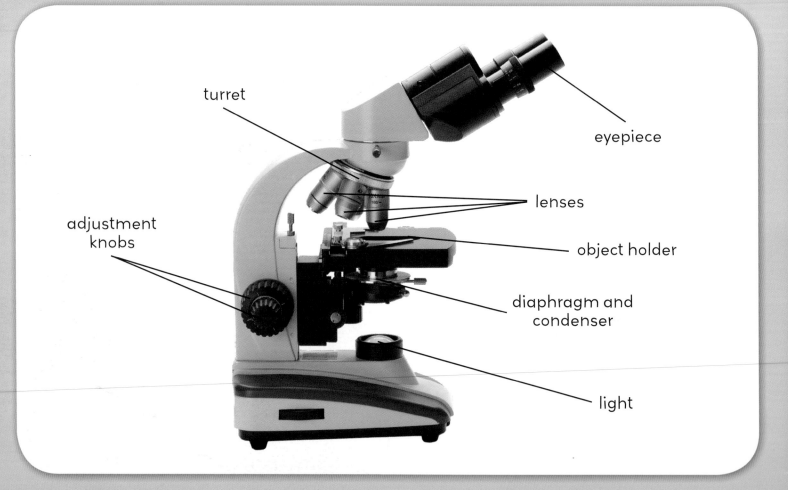

turret

eyepiece

lenses

adjustment
knobs

object holder

diaphragm and
condenser

light

A microscope is used to look at very small things.

The scientist puts something on the object holder under a lens. Then the scientist looks through the eyepiece. The lens makes the object look much larger than it is.

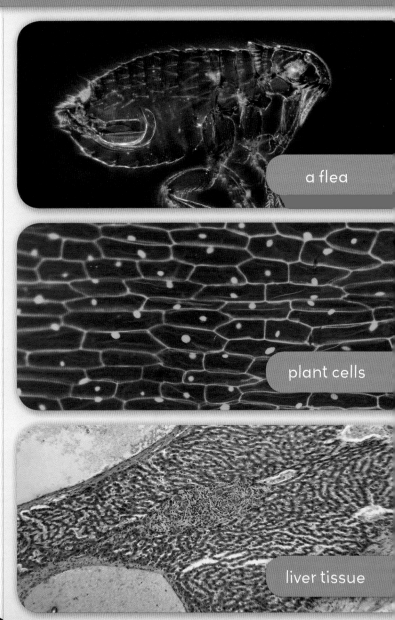

a flea

plant cells

liver tissue

Jenny wants to cure a **disease**. She looks at a **tissue sample** under a microscope.

Karen is learning biology. She studies plant **cells** under a microscope.

GLASSWARE

Erlenmeyer flask

test tube

beaker

graduated cylinder

Erlenmeyer flask

graduated cylinder

filtering flask

250 ml

200

150

100

50 ml

40 ml APPROX

30

20

0 25
ml ml
2 23
4 21
6 19
8 17
10 15
12 13

125 ml

100

75

50

Glassware is used to hold and measure chemicals.

The top and bottom of a beaker are about the same size.

The bottom of a flask is wider than its top.

A graduated cylinder is tall and thin.

A test tube is a thin tube with a round bottom.

Cynthia is doing an experiment with her mom.
She puts a red liquid in a test tube.

Angie, Simon, and Peter are mixing chemicals.
They are using flasks and beakers.

OPTICAL TELESCOPE

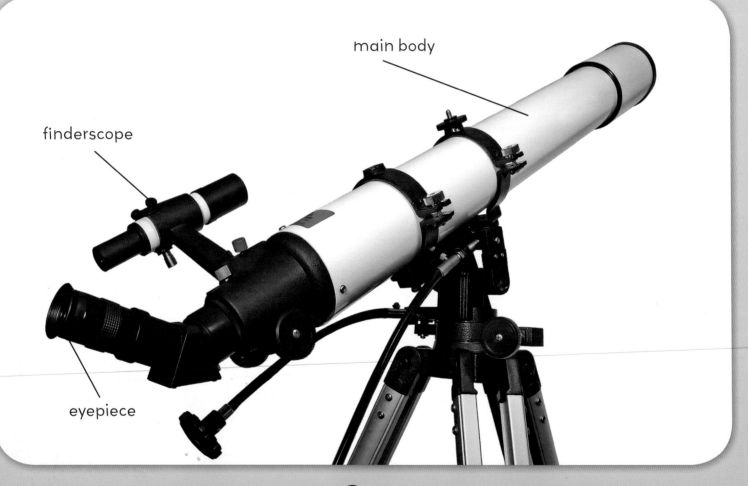

main body

finderscope

eyepiece

Optical telescopes are used to see objects that are far away.

An optical telescope has either **mirrors** or lenses inside it. Light enters the body of the telescope. The light hits the mirrors or lenses. Then it goes to the eyepiece.

The lenses make far away objects look close.

Zach got a telescope for his birthday.
He uses it to look at the moon.

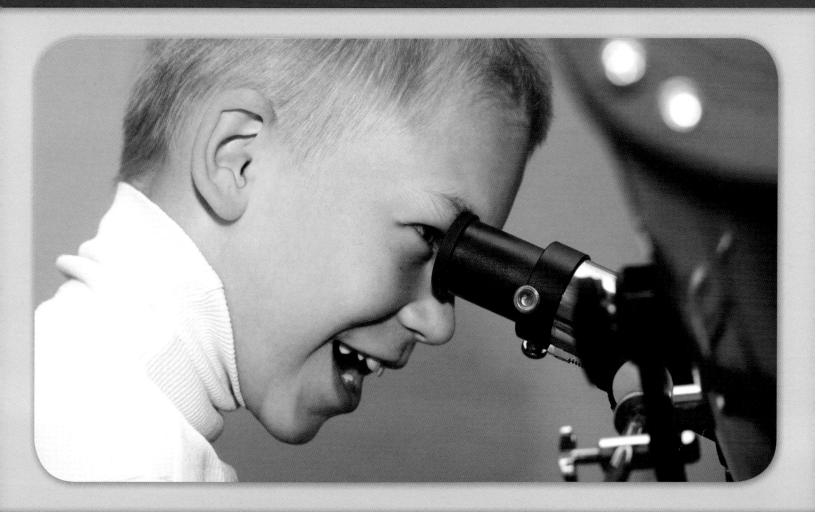

**Brandon's class is visiting an observatory.
It's Brandon's turn to look through the telescope.**

RADIO TELESCOPE

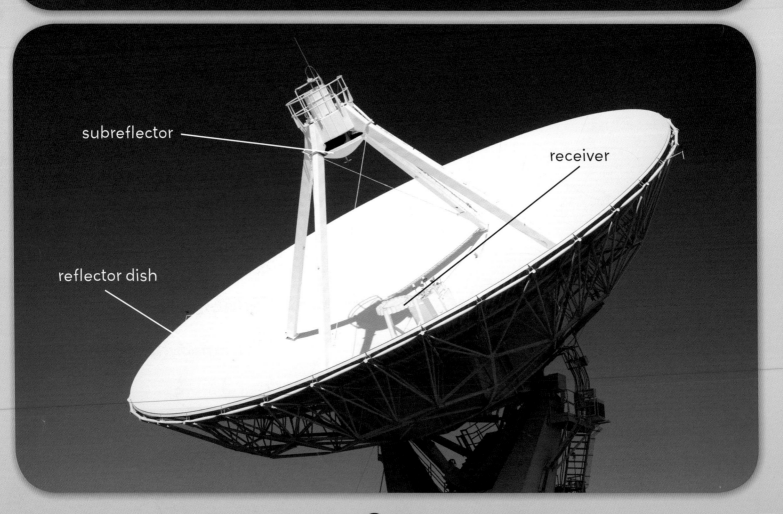

subreflector

receiver

reflector dish

A radio telescope senses radio waves from outer space.

Space objects such as the sun, **galaxies**, and **supernovas** send out radio waves. A radio telescope records these radio waves.

The radio waves can be turned into images. Astronomers study the images to learn about the objects in space.

The Arecibo Observatory is the largest single-dish telescope. It is 1,000 feet (305 m) across.

The Very Large Array is a radio observatory in New Mexico. It has 27 radio telescopes.

MATCH THE WORDS TO THE PICTURES!

The answers are on the bottom of the page.

MATCH GAME

1. optical telescope

a.

2. microscope

b.

3. radio telescope

c.

4. glassware

d.

TEST YOUR TOOL KNOWLEDGE!

The answers are on the bottom of the page.

1.

A microscope makes objects look smaller than they are.

TRUE OR FALSE?

2.

The top of a flask is wider than its bottom.

TRUE OR FALSE?

3.

An optical telescope is used to see objects that are far away.

TRUE OR FALSE?

4.

A radio telescope records radio waves.

TRUE OR FALSE?

TOOL QUIZ

Answers: 1) false 2) false 3) true 4) true

cell – a part of a person, animal, or plant that is too small for the eye to see.

disease – a sickness.

galaxy – a very large group of stars, planets and other objects in space. The Earth is in a galaxy called the Milky Way.

goggles – large glasses that fit tightly over your eyes to protect them.

mirror – a polished or smooth surface, such as glass, that reflects images.

orbit – to move in a circular path around something.

supernova – when a star explodes and gives off more light than the sun.

tissue sample – a group of similar cells that form one part of a plant or animal.